Diary of a Super Spy 3: A Giant Problem!

Peter Patrick

William Thomas

What happens on the mission, stays on the mission...

Diary of a Super Spy 3: A Giant Problem!

Peter Patrick

William Thomas

Copyright © 2015

Published by Run Happy Publishing

Also in the series:

Diary of a Super Spy

Diary of a Super Spy 2: Attack of the Ninjas!

Diary of a Super Spy 4: Space!

Chapter 1

School Camp

Oh, the life of being a super spy in the sixth grade.

I know what you're thinking – it must be all thrills and excitement.

Well, it's not.

Even though you save the world and battle nasty enemies, you still have to do all the normal sixth grade stuff.

Like go to school camp.

Ugh.

I love the outdoors but the idea of running around with the rest of the sixth grade for three days doesn't thrill me. In fact, it scares me a little. Anything can go wrong...

My name is Charlie Chucky, I'm in the sixth grade and I love to jump over anything dangerous.

This is me jumping over a massive, dangerous puddle of water.

My best friend Harley has also come on the school camp.

This is Harley.

As you can tell, Harley doesn't like the outdoors.

To make this boring camp more interesting, I snuck some of Dad's newest gadgets into my backpack.

My Dad is a super spy.

And not just any super spy – he is the world's best super spy. He works for a spy agency so secret that even he doesn't know the name of it.

He battles bad guys and saves the world on a weekly basis but is still home for dinner most nights.

Recently, he has been helping me learn how to become a future super spy.

He even let me go to the 'International Spy Building' where he works. I was stoked about that.

After we have set up our beds at the camp, I sneak out with Harley and show him all the cool stuff I brought in my backpack.

"What's that?" Harley asks as I pull out the first gadget.

"It's the latest type of mini gun," I respond.

"It's so super small. What does it do? Does it blow things up like a bomb?"

"Nope. It does the opposite. This mini gun shrinks things."

"Shrinks things? Like what I do when Mom puts a plate of hot dogs in front of me?"

"No Harley. The number of hot dogs on the plate shrinks because you eat them."

"Ha. Yeah. Good point."

"This mini gun would shrink a plate of normal size hot dogs into a tiny bowl of tiny little hot dogs."

"Why would you want to do that? That's a stupid gun. Who would want to eat tiny little hot dogs?" Harley looks at me confused.

"No Harley. This mini gun isn't supposed to shrink hot dogs. It's supposed to shrink bad guys!"

"Oh... right. Yep. That makes sense."

"And check this out!" I pull out Dad's newest gadget.

"Cool. A helmet with glasses," Harley is stoked.

"Invisible things? Like what? I've never seen anything invisible before."

"That's because it's invisible!"

"Oh right. Yeah. That's some cool stuff Charlie. You might need it with that forest over there."

We both turn to look at the forest next to our camp.

Who would build a school camp next to the strangest, creepiest, spookiest, darkest forest in the world?

"I heard that people go into the forest and don't come back out," Harley whispers.

"That's stupid," I tell Harley, "Nobody can get stuck in a forest forever."

It is the middle of a hot and sweaty day but the forest still looks dark and cold.

That is well scary.

There is something wrong with that place...

Chapter 2

The Forest

Once everyone in the sixth grade has settled into camp, the camp leaders make us play a soccer game against each other. There are three camp leaders for the sixth grade and they are way too cheerful. They look like the smiles have been painted on their faces. They'll probably get jobs as clowns when they grow up.

Jack the Jock, Jim the Jump and Jon the Jingle totally dominate the soccer game. I get to kick the ball twice but that is as much action as I see.

Those three guys train for sport every night of the week. Sometimes I wonder if they even sleep. They probably go to bed a eight o'clock, wake up at midnight and start doing push-ups, sit-ups and squats until it is time to go back to school where they play sport at every opportunity. They even tried to play baseball in Mr. Pale's science class.

Mr. Pale didn't like his ruler being used as a baseball bat but it was when they used his pet frog as a catcher that he really got angry.

Halfway through the soccer game, the ball goes close to Harley.

Harley is a nice kid but he is one of the least sporty kids in the grade. To my surprise, he kicks the ball.

But he doesn't just kick the ball.

He kicks it hard!

Real hard.

Like he was trying to punish the ball for going so close to him.

And the ball goes flying.

And flying...

And flying...

The whole class watches the ball go sailing way over our heads, way over the goals and way over the camp.

It keeps flying and bounces once... straight into the creepy forest.

Everyone freezes.

In the sixth grade, all the boys think they are tough. Nobody wants to say they are scared of some little dark forest.

But it is clear that we are all scared.

Expect for Jack the Jock.

He happily chases the ball right into the forest. He probably isn't scared because he wouldn't even know what scary is. I would be surprised if he could spell it too. All he cares about is sport, sport, sport, butterflies, sport and sport.

Jack the Jock is usually very quick at anything he does. He is built for speed. He is quick into the forest but he takes a very long time to get the ball.

The forest is so dark that I can't even see him in there.

How long does it take to get a ball?

Is the ball stuck in a tree or something?

Maybe he tripped over?

It is pretty dark in there.

Or maybe something else happened...

The whole sixth grade waits for Jack the Jock to come out of the forest with the ball...

And we wait...

And wait...

And wait...

But he doesn't come back out.

We call out for him but there is no answer.

What is in that forest?

The campsite leader pretends to be brave and goes into the forest to find Jack the Jock, but he doesn't come back out either.

Oh no...

Chapter 3

Going into the Forest...

When Jack the Jock and the campsite leader don't return out of the forest, the rest of the camp leaders argue about who will go into the forest next.

The whole sixth grade starts to look worried. We need to save Jack the Jock. He is the only reason our school wins any sporting event.

But nobody wants to go in.

"We need someone really brave to go in there," Mia says to the camp leaders.

Mia is the prettiest girl in school. Even at school camp, she looks like a Hollywood actress. I try not to think about her much, but every night she seems to come into my dreams.

In my dream last night, she was a princess eating ice cream at a fancy restaurant and I was an astronaut who asked her if I could walk her dog. Strange dream.

"I'll do it," I say loudly.

What?

Why would I say that?

I don't know why I said that. I don't really want to go into the forest. Actually, I don't want to go in there at all. I'm scared of the forest. Real scared.

"What?" Harley whispers to me.

"And Harley will come with me," I announce to the rest of the sixth grade.

Harley's eyes almost pop out of his head. Harley isn't brave. He gets scared when his Mom takes away his favourite teddy bear. I saw him at lunchtime yesterday sitting in a corner and I asked him what was wrong. He said, 'I'm so scared. I was thinking about a world without chocolate.'

Actually, that is pretty scary.

"You're so brave," Mia smiles to me.

Wow. She has a great smile.

"Just come with me," I whisper to Harley, "Mia will think that we are really brave."

"But we're not brave," Harley whispers back.

"That doesn't matter. There's nothing to be scared of. It's just a forest. How bad can it be?"

"It could be full of monsters, or ghosts, or trees!"

"Um… yep. I think it is full of trees," I say as Harley looks really nervous, "But don't worry Harley. I'll bring the gadgets with my backpack."

Harley doesn't know how to say no.

So he says yes.

We walk into the dark forest and it is well scary.

Definitely the scariest place I have ever been. It is dark, cold and full of stuff I can't see.

I try to be brave but it is hard to be brave when you're shaking so much. I take the torch out of my backpack to look for any sign of Jack the Jock or the camp leader.

The wind howls past my ears and I feel a cold shiver go up my spine. The air in the forest is damp and the smell is terrifying. Harley is shaking so much already.

I think I hear a scream ahead of us...

I see a pair of eyes looking at me, but when I shine my torch at it, it disappears.

Ahhh...

I'm sure I feel two spiders run over my legs.

And they feel like big spiders...

I don't want to walk into the forest any further... but I have to be brave and find Jack the Jock.

The branches of the trees reach out to us like long arms and I'm sure this place is haunted.

Oh no...

My heart is beating so fast.

The deeper into the forest we walk, the darker it becomes. I have never been scared of the dark but right now, it frightens me...

I shine my torch ahead and we see the soccer ball stuck in a tree.

"Here's the ball. Let's go now," Harley whispers.

"No, we can't go yet," I say, "We have to find the camp leader and Jack the Jock."

Harley walks behind me, gripping my backpack tightly.

As we walk further into the forest, we hear a noise ahead of us.

A loud, crunching noise.

A scary, loud, crunching noise...

Oh no...

What is it?

Chapter 4

Deep into the Forest

Everything stops when we hear the noise.

My heart is beating so hard!

I grip the torch super tight as I look for anything in the forest. I can't see anything!

What is ahead of us?

I hold my breath as I wait for something to happen...

CRUNCH.

We hear another noise...

CRUNCH.

And another noise...

CRUNCH.

The noises are getting closer to us!

What is coming for us?

I grab Harley and pull him behind a rock to hide.

What is the noise?!

What is in the forest?!

It's the camp leader.

He sprints past us as fast as he can. I don't think I've ever seen anyone run as fast as he is. He could probably break a world record right now.

"Run for your lives!" he yells to us.

And he doesn't stop.

He just keeps running.

"Maybe we should listen to him?" Harley asks me, "I mean, he is the camp leader after all. If he says that we should run for our lives, maybe we should do what we're told?"

"No Harley," I shake my head, "We still have to find Jack the Jock."

We come out from behind the rock and keep walking into the dark forest...

And then - the dark forest stops. We come to a clearing up ahead.

"See," I tell Harley, "There is nothing to be afraid of."

"Look! There's Jack the Jock," Harley says as we stare at the clearing.

Jack the Jock is lying in the middle of the grass clearing.

"What happened to him?" Harley asks me.

"I don't know but he looks like he has been knocked out."

Harley starts to run towards him.

"Wait," I stop Harley from going any further, "I have a bad feeling about this."

Chapter 5

Saving Jack the Jock

Jack the Jock has been knocked out cold.

Standing at the edge of the clearing, we call out to him but he doesn't answer. Jack the Jock looks like he has been hit by something but there is nothing around him.

"I can't see anything," Harley says, "Whatever hit him must have left already."

"I don't think so Harley. Something about this seems odd."

Harley ignores me and starts to walk towards Jack the Jock on the ground.

"Harley, wait…"

But Harley keeps walking.

And then…

WHACK!

Harley is hit by something and he goes flying!

When he lands, he is knocked out cold, lying next to Jack the Jock.

I can't see anything!

I stare into the clearing but I can't see what hit Harley!

What is going on?!

I take another look but I still can't see anything... and then it occurs to me.

Something invisible must be out there!

An invisible thing must have hit Jack the Jock and Harley!

I pull open my backpack and put on my invisible glasses...

Oh no...

This is not good...

Chapter 6

The Problem

With my invisible glasses on, I can see everything.

Standing in front of me are four of the biggest, ugliest, meanest looking giants I have ever seen. Not that I've seen a lot of giants.

But did I mention that these ones are huge and invisible!

As soon as the shock subsides, one of the giants spots me. He doesn't look like he is in the mood for sitting down and having a long chat about pop music with a can of soda. Nope. He actually looks like he is in the mood to eat me for dinner.

"Hey guys, who wants to hear a joke?" I try to reason with them.

They don't respond.

"What's higher than a giant?"

No response.

"A giant's hat!" I laugh.

Yeah, I have never been great at telling jokes.

"Did you hear about the giant who sneezed?" I continue, "It was all over town…"

The giants don't laugh. I think that the jokes have made them angrier!

Oops.

Time for Plan B…

RUN!

As I run under the giant's legs, I realize how tall he is.

Not basketball player tall like Leaping Larry in the sixth grade – nope, these giants are more Empire State Building sort-of-tall.

I can't defeat four giants this tall!

I can't even reach their toes!

I'm doomed!

Why did I even go into the forest in the first place?

But then I remember what's in my backpack!

I have a shrinking gun!

Quickly, I pull the mini gun out of my backpack and aim at the first giant.

ZAP!

Yes! What a great shot!

This shrinking gun rocks! Instantly, the first invisible giant shrinks to mini size!

Awesome!

My giant problem has just become a mini problem!!

ZAP!

I turn and shoot another giant!

This shrinking gun is so awesome!

ZAP!

And fun!

When I get home, I'm going to shrink the neighbor's stupid big, barking dog that always tries to eat my school shorts.

As I turn to shoot the last giant...

Trip!

I trip over one of the mini giants!

When I fall, my helmet goes flying away from me!

Oh no!

I try to reach for my helmet again but it has fallen too far away!

Without my helmet, I can't see the last invisible giant!

Where is he?

He remains at large!

He could be anywhere!

I try to reach the helmet again but...

Suddenly, the last invisible giant grabs me...

I'm doomed....

Chapter 7

Wrestling a Giant

I'm ruined.

This giant will eat me for sure. Invisible giants are always hungry.

"Charlie!" I hear a voice below.

It's Mia.

"How are you flying?" she asks, as she can't see the invisible giant.

"I'm not flying," I yell as I struggle against the giant.

"Then what are you doing up there?"

If I told Mia that I am about to be eaten by a huge, scary invisible giant – she would think I'm crazy!

"Um… let's just say I have a giant problem right now!" I yell, "I need you to throw up my helmet and my mini gun!"

Quickly, Mia grabs my helmet and mini gun, and throws them up to me.

I put the helmet on...

Whoa!

The giant is about to eat me!

Swiftly, I grab my shrinking gun and I fire a shot straight into his mouth!

"Eat this!" I yell.

ZAP!

Woo!

The last giant shrinks to mini size where it is no longer dangerous!

Phew... that was close!

I laugh as I watch the four mini giants run away from me.

"What are you laughing at Charlie?" Mia looks at me like I'm crazy.

"Um..." I realize that Mia can't see the mini giants, "Nothing."

"And what is with that crazy helmet?" she laughs.

Chapter 8

The Wind

After the mini giants have run back into the dark forest, I turn to Mia to say thanks for throwing up the helmet and mini gun.

"What happened?" she asks, looking confused.

"It was... it was just the wind."

"The wind?" she doesn't believe me, "The wind picked you up and swung you around like that?"

"Yeah, just the wind," I lie.

Mia smiles at me.

She knows I've done something cool but she doesn't know what it is.

"You're alright Charlie Chucky," she smiles, "And you look a lot better without that silly helmet on."

The problem with being a super spy is that you can never tell anyone about all the cool stuff you do. You can never tell anyone that you just saved the day, and you definitely can't tell the school's cutest girl that you've just shrunk four invisible giants.

She would think I'm crazy.

Jack the Jock and Harley begin to wake up, and we help them to their feet.

"What happened?" Jack the Jock asks.

"When you were running, you fell over a stick," I reply.

"A stick? That's not good. I'll have to do more agility drills tomorrow to make sure I don't do that again."

We walk back through the dark forest, find the soccer ball and return to the school camp.

Although Mia doesn't know what I did, I'm sure she thinks I'm cool now.

All in a days work for a super spy, I guess...

The End

Also in the Series:

Made in the USA
San Bernardino, CA
09 November 2015